Soul Kisses

By: Pamela "RareEpiphany" Best

Copyright © 2014

By: Pamela Best

All rights are reserved to the author. No part of this book may be used or reproduced in any manner whatsoever without written permission except in the case of brief quotations embodied in critical articles or reviews.

ISBN 978-0-615-97182-7

This is ...

4Renalone

Preface

This is the book that almost never was. I debated for a long time about publishing this particular body of work. I never really shared *this* kind of poetry with anyone. I kept this side of my skill set pretty hush-hush…except for a few peaks given to close friend and a short section in my last book. Erotic poetry is not what is expected from me.

But you know what…. I got tired of hearing soft porn posturing as sensuality. I read and heard so much vulgarity surrounding something so beautiful, that I felt moved to do something…to write something…to step INside my comfort zone and paint the picture of what love making looks like through my eyes. I take joy in the tease…the promise of things to come. It was my intension to capture as many of the facets of physical love as possible. Is this book vulgar? I don't think so. Is this book nasty? Well that all depends on the context with which you use that word. Is this book highly sensual and insanely erotic?. Absolutely. Hopefully, I've captured just a bit of the beauty made when love sparks electric between souls. Turn down the lights…grab some candles and soft music…chill.

Passion awaits…

Rare Epiphany

Foreword

"…And when she writes, it becomes a necessary thing to not simply be aware… but be present and be absorbed by every word that is given life by the power of her pen." This is how I once described the experience of reading RareEpiphany's work. At that point I didn't know her. I had no expectation of what awaited me on the other side of that reality. If I had known the scope and breadth of her talent and gift, I would have sought her out, if for no other reason than to broaden my appreciation for the art of poetry.

This is the truth that you will discover for yourself as you turn these pages.

I have had the great pleasure of calling her a friend for a few years now. Over time, I have seen the evolution of her work and witnessed first-hand the maturation of her writing. I watched as the jagged edges of her unfiltered energy became smooth, curved, persuasive intentions. I saw as raw talent grew into cultured and fluid skill.

RareEpiphany has arrived and just as her name would suggest, she is a unique and exquisite burst of awareness that forever changes you.

As you make your way through this book, uncovering the layers of sensuality, love, passion, remembrance, and longing, remember to breathe. Take a moment to feel the carefully selected words wash over you. Revel in the linguistic artistry of lines like:

> *"…And I understand now, black holes,*
> *Because the whole of my black soul*
> *Quakes and implodes*
> *Synergistic overload*
> *My star bursts and slowly dies*
> *And then is reborn through your borning cry…"- Moon (Extensions)*

As a writer myself and as one who aspires to become a poet, my appreciation for words and their power is a sacred and cherished thing. I lend my acclaim and ovation to only those who give meaning to these delicate, overwhelming, and sometimes baffling puzzle pieces. Complex interchangeable things that when carefully put together create a magnificent portrait of depth and beauty.
RareEpiphany is such an artist. This book is such a creation.
Enjoy the journey and remember... take time to breathe.

-One Cannon

Inhale...

Anticipation

I taste you

An indulgence like honey upon my lips

thick and sweet

tempting my tongue from the pillowy confines of my mouth

to savor your decadence

piquing rather than fulfilling my hunger.

Your name..an erotic whisper on my breathe

Writhes in the air between us

Nibbling at the tattered remnants of self-control

That can no longer hold our desire at bay

I crave you

And tonight

I will get my fill

Greet Me…

Greet me with smoldering eyes
That refuse to hide your desires
Let me see fire barely checked in your gaze
Raise the Fahrenheit
'til I just might melt into you
I want you to
Greet me with warm hands
That understand placement and pressure
And their correlation to pleasure
How a firm grip, gentle caress
your thumb tracing the outline of my breast
orchestrate the calm before the storm begins
and then…
Greet me with deep kisses
That elicit exodus of breath
Leave me bereft of protest
'til the whole of me acquiesces to your whim
Lick the rim of my lips before slipping inside to taste my decadence
Leave the evidence of your mouth print on my neck
And chest…
Just…
Greet me

Ice Cream Dream

His warm skin is the color of butterscotch with a hint of cinnamon

Or perhaps cardamom

A sensual treat to complete my butter pecan ice cream fantasy

Easily a feast worthy of my eyes and my palate

His pulse is rapid but steady as the heady scent of dessert and desire

Permeates the air

My "come hither" collides with his "I dare…"

Silently declaring war on inhibition

Tonight our mission is to satiate a hunger that has

Gone on much too long

…our song plays

And he lays waiting as I my fingers scoop

Too much but just enough of the ice cream

Then slide between his full lips letting some

Drip

Onto his chin

And then I bend over to lick him clean

The slow swing of my tongue like a pendulum

Marking that the time has come for pleasure

I pour measured spoonfuls of ice cream on his decadent body

While he breathes heavily from the shock of the cold

But the heat of my gaze serves to raise his temperature quickly

And then I lick-y all that sweet stick-y and he's getting thick..he

Wants to dick me… down…

But we won't get around to that 'til round 3 or 4

Round 1 is about adoring his flesh

Hell I'm still dressed and ain't broke a sweat just yet

I'm just having ice cream and I swear it seems I can taste the praline of his skin

As I delight in each shudder and moan and I won't leave him alone until

Every single drop is gone

And he blesses me with the cream I seek that only he can supply

The kind that quenches my deepest sensual appetite.

The Mountains...
~A dedication to those who love to love Beautiful Voluptuous Women~

He said

"I love the mountains"

And my passion muddled mind just couldn't find the meaning

As he loved me insane, I was screaming his name

and his constant refrain

Echoed again

"I love...the mountains"

Between licks and sucks

That made my hips buck and grind

His tongue trekked, sublime, a trail across my

Belly. It was there he smiled and looked at me

And repeated that he...

Loved...the mountains

And the valleys

And every nook and cranny

Of my flesh;

Each ripple and roll

That he could unfold to find hidden treasures of chocolate brown skin

The places that I'd hidden my shame in

Where I'd tucked long lost desires to be thin in

Unlike other men, he reveled in my thickness

Found bliss in the width and girth of my waistline

Dined on a feast of fattening decadence

Devouring all evidence of self consciousness

With him, it's just…

The journey that matters

More than the destination though we'll both get there with patience

In due time

He wants to find new pathways to pleasure

in the dunes and expanse of my desert

linger in my oasis that is soft and warm and wet

'til I forget the insults and innuendos from those

Who didn't know how beautiful it could be in the wilderness of me

He whispered

"I love…the mountains"

as I wrapped my legs around him

and brace for the chaos he has loosed

I can no longer hold back my cries

And I fall quickly to the other side when in my ear

He moans…"baby…I love *you* too"

Mental Picture

Sweet morning kisses

tenderly tasting flavors

of last night's love feast

Mind Grindin'

You seem like the kind of man

that can treat a woman like a lady

but maybe tonight

I want to be treated like your girl

...there's a world of difference

and while I freely admit

that I wish to lick tears from your eyes

as I ride you

slow-ly

and drape me lavishly across your body

Please believe that it's your mind-flow

that got my nose open

and I'm hoping that you'll open my soul wide

and slide your thoughts inside

pushing deep into my mind

with a prolific poetic slow grind

and find my spot

that dot of space that you can hit

and erase all my past lives

all those past lies

all those past ties

to untruths I courted in my youth

Mind-f*ck me 'til I buck free

of the shackles that bind me

'til I beg for mercy cause your verbs are killing me

with their steady in and out

'til I shout multi-syllabic adjectives like they were expletives

and scream superlatives never-minding my fricatives

or plosives

exposed is my very core

when I plead for more and you explore my intellect

with your silver tongue

plunge into me lyrically like a delicacy

Rewriting me with long deliberate strokes

and I spoke you in metaphors

repeat you like the "nevermore"

from Poe's raven

Brazenly cravin' your di-dac-dic....

flow

It grows more rigid the more you give it to me

I see moonflowers as I devour every utterance of your mouth

your down-south skillz got me head over heals

stanzas building to crescendo verses laced with innuendo

you throw your back into it as you spew fluid word-music

and I lose it and scream…I lose it and cream ink all over my sheets

of loose-leaf

you released soliloquies that dripped from me like honey

You've done me and I am complete

and my heart beats a melody for you

my mouth pants a rhythmic groove

and my shaking fingers grasp your bic

my tongue flicks the tip …I tighten my grip

dip my hips and with a

slip of my wrist

I twist limericks

between lip-licks

pulling hat tricks with quick-witted precision

like a piston until you blast ink in a passionate blink of my 3rd eye and I try not to spill a drop but it drips

from my lips in the sweetest haiku's

and doiditsu's spew forth like summer rain

can't contain those triolets

that got me wet and kyrielles keep me in a

purple haze

we make it do what it do

and I got the sweetest love jones for making poetry

With you

Lick
~(**HAND**LE)~

You watch me;

read the story unfolding behind my eyes;

take note of every twitch of my jaw

…quiver of my lips;

Studying, diligently, every subtle nuance of

My flesh…My breathing…My voice

Your touch

Responds to my call

Slowly…gently playing me

Like a maestro on piano

You quicken…when my body beckons

Then, mastering me, you

Take control of my rhythm

Directing…Guiding…Soliciting…

The look…sound…movement you want

Coaxing me to the brink

Teetering on the edge 'til I beg

But you don't let me fall…yet

You watch me;

the masterpiece before you

a living breathing portrait of passion

then you…push me over into ecstasy

spread my thighs

…sigh

And then

~Lick~

Body Music

Last night we made body music

limbs entangled

dancing to the steady

suck/slide rhythm

of hips in overdrive

accented by the percussive scratching of sheets

springs singing staccato to the

headboard's driving kick

made perfect by the syncopated knocks of

neighbors on walls

begging for decrescendo

but artisans that we are,

we…

Da Capo

From the beginning again

this time legato

tonguing each note expertly

bringing in congo lines

charmed hips subtly

undulate

churning; churning

it's butter baby

hands sliding along ribcage

fingers caressing each bone like

harp strings

or more like

keys on a baby grand

and baby damn how you

play so smooth and slow

the barely audible grip of fingers on moist skin

fades into the whisper soft backdrop

of sighs and moans

then warm licked lips

slip low and play my flute

rubato

driving hard to crescendo

tongue conducts slow arching of back

salsa y meringue

throaty alto once dolce

now rings Sforzando

this is body music

and tears flow and

alto modulates to sharp soprano

then

~consonance~

found in the ragged breaths of 2 musicians

finally completing

lovers' brown-skinned symphony

Body Kiss

Warm lips lingering

On soft, sun-kissed mocha skin

Savoring heaven

He's Cumming For Me

Right now…it doesn't matter If the sky shatters

or stars scatter like confetti to the ground

I've found peace in the space between

his moans and the earth-tones of our damp skin

something akin to tribal dances advance from our hips

and we take slow sips of lust

and if right now I be thrust into an ever after missing the chapters

to a happy ending

I'll still be sending candy kisses to the sun

because the one thing that does matter

is that he's cumming for me

and I can see the eminent arrival in his eyes

and the way he grips my thighs tells me he's close

and the most beautiful sound escapes his throat

and I feel the remote trembling that emanates from a place

so primitive and deep that it reaches peaks at rock bottoms

Autumn's turned to spring and everything cold is now hot

and I forgot the meaning of the universe when he softly

cursed the wave about to overtake him and me

and history is repeating itself and self control is beating itself and I don't give a damn cause I am weathering the storm

in the safety of his arms and

he's cumming for me

white waters run rapidly

tempos increase and I succumb to the slow heat

of his piston-like motions

drowning his steel adrenaline in my sticky wet ocean

he takes me fast and hard

threatening to rip me apart but my heart won't let me stop

reaching desperately for that mountain top

and it doesn't matter that my mind's locked in a pleasure-pain trap

and it doesn't matter that my body lies at the brink of collapse

or that in the distance my fragile soul hears strains of taps

What does matter is the faint quiver of his lips

and the way he pants in steady succinct sips

and I squeeze my thighs tightly around his hips

and rock my backside in the jagged rhythm of his grip

He is cumming for me and that reality

rivals my every fantasy and I am happy to be there

when he arrives

Dream Only Today

I do not profess to be pure

My body's endured the lusts of a few

But for you...I've resigned my sexuality

To celibacy because, for me,

There is only you

And old fading flames just won't do

I'm going to be honest

When I lie in my bed at night

Staring off into the darkness

My heart is beating your name

And as my hands caress my frame

It's your touch I am longing for

And when I whisper "more"

I hope the night winds pour it in your ears

And somehow from 783 miles away you will hear my plea

And maybe through telepathy acquiesce

Ren I confess that I...I read your poetry

And consequently my fingers may linger on my skin too long

And when on the phone I sometimes masturbate to the unsteady shake of your sigh

And you wonder why I'm often quiet on the line

Cause I'm hiding the fact that in my mind…I'm screaming your name

While sliding into my wetlands over and over again

And I sometimes giggle when I imagine how your tongue tickles

When you

Kiss

Lick

…..Suck

my nipples

desire ripples through me like your breath raining on my chocolate stream

seems surreal when I can feel your kisses

and I'm suppressing hisses and sighs and I really really try

to say your name without tasting it on my tongue

because right now your name aches in me to be sung

like praises

my mouth braces and I utter

ren

...r-ren

uhm...rennnn

but like butter, it melts on my lips

and my passion drips down my chin

making my intentions hard to hide

baby I want you inside me

deeply

wrapping me in ecstasy

I want to look deeply in your eyes

As you ride my waves and I don't want to be saved from

The seismic activity ripping through me with each stroke

I want you soaked in my juices

Finding my elusive g-spot

Til what was hot is now boiling over

Then turn me over and infuse your being into my cellular memory

Let every shimmering bead of sweat beget a story of the glory

Of the things we did to each other

Ren...in my dreams, you're already my lover

And I've already tasted every inch of you

Done things most are ashamed to do

Had the skin beneath my nails tell the tale

Of the scars on your back

Had my azz smacked until it was warm and red

Fed you honey str8 from my comb

And made the space between your thighs as much a home

As I've made the space behind your eyes

I've sighed your name for hours on end

'til my neighbors all know that my body belongs to Ren

and they tell me…That man must be puttin' it down

not knowing that you're not even around

it sounds foolish

but I make no prudish claims of sweetness

you are my weakness

and I don't want to be strong

just lay languidly replete after making love to you all night long

"O"

Sweet; honeyed moans bloom
Leaving the aroma of
Your name on my breath

Good Love

His stroke...is music
Painting me with melody
From the inside out

Dare…

"Truth or dare?"

Well most are aware that I never

Back down from a challenge

Even when I know I'm going to lose

See I choose to feed my *need* for a little

Friendly competition

Admissions…?

They're just not my thing , I mean considering

I'm already an open book so I look into

Those *sultry* eyes the color of cognac

And shoot back…"Dare"

And the *intensity* of his intentions permeated the air

Yeah….I was in trouble

But I took a double dose of "f**k it" and stuck it out

'Cause see, something about his eyes and the quickening rise and fall of his chest

Made me *acquiesce* to his every demand

So when he took my hands and raised them above my head

Secured the handcuffs and held me *taut* against the bed

I said...not a mumbling syllable

Just let the visuals speak for me...

Licked my full lips as evidence that my thoughts

Were devoid of *innocence*

Gave him a look that sent his pulse point racing

He began tracing an *intricate* pattern along my thigh

And sighed all the nasty things he was gonna do to me

And the dare you see...

Well he dared me to let him in

Not just my body

But he wanted my soul...

My *whole*

Dared me to relinquish control and in the *absence*

Of pretense and hindrance

Just let go

And you know

that I never

Back down from a challenge

Even when I know I may not win

But in the end, love has no losers

Only better educated contestants who are destined

To love again if things don't blend the first time around

So I bound my heart to his like he'd bound my hands to the bed

…tightly…

Then said

I will.

Only Just Begun

I tried to speak

But the words caught in my throat and my breath

Wrote/Hummed your name in a song

That depicted whom it/I belong to

And you...you listened intently

Bent me to your whim and will with

The stillness of your gaze

Moved my heart in so many ways

Here, in your embrace

I am amazed by the taste of your lips

That I trace with nimble tongue

And it has only just begun, my love

We have only

Just begun

*white lace and promises

A kiss for luck and we're on our way...

Soar

He said
"close your eyes"
And I…I…I… was afraid…
afraid that he would make me
Lose control
And control…was all I had
Then he took the pads of his finger….
Made an arduous lingering trek along my thigh
Let the heat of his sigh melt my resistance
As his touch danced bolero then merengue on my skin
He said….again
"close your eyes"
….and the melodious moan in his voice
Gave me no other choice
But to obey
My salient heart almost visible through bone and flesh
'til he meshed his fingers in mine
And slowed down time with a kiss…
That effortlessly comforted me
The way he licked then sucked
My lips like their delicious decadence
Dripped of living water…as if I was daughter of the Nile
And He, Solomon
I was undone when he said
"now with your minds eye….
Take these hands of mine…

And let me show you how…to fly"
…and I …
Soar

Long Kiss Goodnight

He loved me clit-orally

I mean…literally

Licked lavish love songs of longing and belonging

Between my thighs and

Between my sighs

He'd speak an aphorism or a steady rhythm of words like

"Lost time is never found again"

So he made the most of his by going down again

And when I couldn't remember my name between orgasmic fits

He said "those who cannot remember the past, are condemned to repeat it"

Like his clit licks….like his clit licks…like his clit licks…like one's foot slips

On the sustain pedal of a piano

My alto now rang soprano

Though I tried not to expose how I was about to explode

But how could he not know that he was about to overthrow

My queendom

He'd become the only one to take my power

But this rare flower didn't use it against me

He used it to free me

From the fear that our love was infatuation

In disguise

But his eyes couldn't lie and

this lovemaking exemplified the truth of us

this wasn't lust

just icing on the cake….like my release on his face

and the warmth of his embrace when he's finished

this long kiss…goodnight

Home ~ The Deep Down Of Me

It started in the

Deep down of me

The deep warm brown of me

Where none but love and your lust can touch.

To whom much is given

Much is required

And I aspire to open myself

Ocean wide

Then you can slide into

The deep down of me

The deep warm brown of me

And get off on the sound of me

Ushering you inside of me with praises

While my face is the picture of passion

And my hips skillfully fashioned to take it

How you give it

~Deep~

Down

Past the

Brown of me

In the very black of me

Damn near middle passage savagery

or could it be

~plantation relations~

when you loved like it was the last time

cause it could very well be the last time.

My fingers clutch your spine and

I breathe in sync with yo grind

And the only thing on my mind

Is 'please daddy take yo time'

And find the

Deep

So deep

Down brown of me

So I can cry yo name

When you're deep inside of me

And you'll know without doubt that you have found in me

A place called home.

The Morning After

A smile plays on my lips
Legato….
Taking it's time before resting lightly on my heart
I remember
Wanton whispers wistfully washing over sacred secrets
You spoke a language
That only skin and breath
Understood intimately
And I ,now, crave the fluency of
Your tongue

SuperNova

It was

Half past midnight

when darkness shattered like black glass

unable to withstand high decibel declarations of dayum near perfect love making

my mouth shone naked against the sky

a full moon

howling at itself

Rhythms crests

and stars, ignited by passion's flame,

incinerate.

Robbed of breathe,

sensations collapse into themselves

and implode

now I be supernova

brilliantly scattered

gleaming stardust in your eyes

and you cry angels wings

fluttering light against my cheek

seeking refuge in my ear

tapping tympanic love songs

that reverberate through my bones

to my soul;

to my whole.

Letting me know that love

Has no language

Save the stroke of your fingers in my hair

And the warm wet of your kiss on my skin

in these late night sessions I learn object lessons

that carry me through my days

so I can make it to dusk

and hear the faint flutter of angels wings

finding serenity in knowing

he will make me his star again tonight

Memory Lane

I'm travelling back

down

memory lane

to a night in February…68 degrees with light drizzling rain

but inside….it was 100 plus

cause when I'm alone with you

heat and humidity is a must

you just….do that to me

and that night I couldn't have adequately anticipated

the way our feelings would be communicated

it was surreal

the look in your eyes spoke volumes incessantly

the way you touched me whispered you wanted me

as we spoke in tongues with our tongues

entangled

and we dangled dangerously on the edge

of animal behavior

I still taste the salty-sweet flavor

of the nape of your neck

and

still feel the cool trickle of

glistening beads of sweat

I shiver as I recall the soft warmth of your breath snaking down my spine

causing all of my protests to spill off my tongue as whimpers and whines

for…

"…oooh sì…più.. il mio amore"

and I tried so hard to control the trembling that began

in my legs

and I couldn't stop the screams of ecstasy

no matter how fiercely I gripped the bed

Could barely make out your voice in my ear or your

soft, yet demanding invitation to…cum

had no control over the tears that fell as you made

my body hummmm

And when I opened myself wider to receive you deeper

and moaned your name repeatedly in your ear

the low guttural growl that escaped from betwixt your clenched teeth

caused all sanity to disappear

I lost my mind in the grind of your fine as wine hips

I lost my resistance in the insistence and urgency of your lips

I lost my fear and doubt with each in and out on the floor and couch and bed

I lost my association with articulation for there was no translation for what I said

...we were Kinetic – energy in motion

so thoroughly charged that we set off millions of explosions

and I live to tell the story

of love making so intense

that it took me 9 months, 1 week, 3 days and 8 hours

to write anything about it that made any sense

Love Making

dark bodies entwined

breathless whispers of lovers

passion's melody

Afterglow

I cried
passionate tears
as he rocked me sweetly
in warm sticky love-locked embrace
complete

Nights Like This

On nights like this

I dream of

skinny dipping in the amber pools of your eyes

bathing in your gaze and watching son's set on your horizon

I run along your brown sand beaches

enjoying the feel of dampness that comes after

the tearful rains

and on nights like this

I dream of the scent of your warm moist skin

inhale again and again the masculine zen cupped in your collarbone

take slow sips of sweet chocolate

languishing lavish licks on the back of your neck

try hard to keep in check the slow simmer consuming me

and you make it hard, you see, cause you moan my name so

deliciously that I subsequently almost forget to be good

I exhale slowly

as I try to get steady

on my feet

but you greet my retreat with advances

and sensual glances over your shoulder

coupled with hands that grow bolder by the minute

make eminent my demise

what I see in your eyes makes me tremble

and it nimbly removes my inhibitions

as you switch positions to face me

and I see the breadth and depth of your hunger for me

my eyes plead for mercy

but you show none

and I'm undone as I slowly run my hands over your chest

let them rest on your ribcage as I engage

in slow, sensual, French kisses

on our nipples

desire ripples through your body

pinning me between a rock and a

very hard place

brace for the tidal waves about to hit my shore

as bodies hit floor

I scream for more

while on all fours

Am shaken to my core

and honey love pours all over us

just melting into molten pools of pleasure

...and

On nights like this

I dream that your kiss

fixes all of my broken places

fills all of my empty spaces

and erases all those bad memories etched on the walls of my soul

It's nights like this

when halves are made whole

It's nights like this when dreams come true

and on nights like this

I dream

about you

Can You Handle Me (The Reply)

You asked me a question

And my most honest confession

Is that you already know the answer

But perhaps I can enhance your memory

You ask "Can you please me"

My answer…absolutely…completely

See

You bring out the primitive in me

That lives and breathes to pleasure thee

I'm fully focused man

And understand that I don't make empty promises

Honest is the depth and breadth of my skill

Warm breath on your neck sending chills down your spine

Taking my time to so thoroughly f*ck your mind

That your pump is primed and flowing

Without you knowing what hit you

And I ain't even touched you…yet

And I bet you never knew you could

Speak patwah or experience the power of binwah

Or have a ménage a' trois with just two

Can I please you?

Give me something harder to do

Need I remind you of the slow sips of zen

My tongue wrenched from your collar bone?

Or playful chuckles my touch turned into deep indiscriminate moans?

My hands and mouth will meet every inch or your skin

Before you ever get to slide into my silk chocolate treasure

And if you never knew how many licks it takes to get

To the center of your tootsie roll….

Then hold your breath and take note

Cause my deep throat will cause remote

Earthquakes in the center of your universe

Dams will burst and preacha's will curse and

Call God's name in the same sentence

(thank and praise him for repentance

cause you gon' need it)

And can you believe it's only just begun?

And I'm still dressed hon'

And this is only chapter one

Of the novel I want to inscribe in cuneiform

Upon the brown clay tablet of your skin?

So enough with the questions

Let's deal with the answers

As for pleasure…

The answer is yes

Unequivocally, Undoubtedly, Most definitely

I deliver

Just make sure your quiver is full and ready

'cause my deep down body thirst…is near deadly

and I ain't had a drink in a long time

so now Graham Central's question is mine

Can you handle it?

Can You Handle

…me?

Fly

Strong hands grip wayward hips

As back arches; bends deep

Connecting pain and pleasure

beautifully

I dance

Curved like ballerinas' feet

Riding your upward thrusts

Like ocean waves

I rock

And roll

Bowed like double bass bridge

Your fingers on my frets

You play me spicatto

The vibration of my strings making me sing

And Crescendo

I sway and shake with each seismic shift

With each pitch and yaw

I hold tighter

Grip harder

Spread my wings

And fly….

Memory Lane ~ The Reprise~

I want to go back down memory lane

where you made golden fire run through my veins

unchained the vixen within

I give in and begin to lick your lips

take slow sips of your tongue

and undo your tie

slide my hands from your hair to your

derriere and tug your shirt tail to unvail

the small of your back

lose track of seconds and hours

as I completely devour your mouth

hands travel south to set you free

and we

moan luscious lullabies

bubbling into passionate cries for release

you eased my dress over my shoulders

and your hands grew bolder as you

caressed my body Braille like a blind man

read my pages over and over again

and I kiss your chin in a slow Sunday afternoon

drive to your thighs

back you up against the wall

lest ye fall from the temptation

and my oral libations bring forth

subtle undulations of your hips as honey molasses

drips in creamy drops but I don't stop

as your hands take firm grasp of hair

and I stare directly into your eyes

relishing in raw sighs that tumble from your

palate like mystic Arabic verses

soft curses of sweet misery

as you watch me watching you

through passion laden eyes and I grip your thighs

and take you farther; deeper into my wonderland of bliss

this most passionate kiss.

and you tell me to wait but I wickedly disobey

as I survey liquid heat pervading your body

and eagerly I drink from your fountain

until sweet waters flow down in my soul

roll my tongue so I miss none

and quench my thirst

first fruits of my labor savored like fine wine

the kind you roll around in your mouth to get the full flavor

and seconds later you join me on the floor for more of that

"...oooh sì...più.. il mio amore"

I'm on all fours looking back at you

as you do that jazzy funky shit that you do when you do

what you do the way you do it to me

got me moaning and whimpering "ooh Papi"

reaching for things that simply aren't there

heat of our passion evaporating my air

calling your name in Portuguese and wild banshee patwah

begging on bated breath "please baby don't stop"

And you don't

but time does

as we make the kind of love

that rocks reality into oblivion

leaving obsidian aftermath

as your lava clears a path to my soul

control my body like I'm on marionette strings

things too graphic to explain

Rain stained window panes

paint kaleidoscopic pictures on the ceiling

revealing the dance that is love

between us...Raw lust mingled with

real affection...Absolute and total perfection

and while I had to wait a while to bless paper with my pen

I'm trying to think up ways to get home to you so we can do it all again.

On My Neck

You lick your lips

Moaning appreciation for

The evening meal….

And I feel…the slow suck/slide drag

Of your mouth on each finger…

The way the tips linger on your bottom lip

While your gaze slips to my breasts and

Despite my best efforts,

The nipples perk up and strain.

I try to regain my composure

So the hostess in me takes over

To clear to table.

I'm barely able to tear my eyes from your gaze.

I make my way to the kitchen to begin the ritual

Of cleaning.

I'm leaning over the sink trying to blink back

Nervous tears

Trying to think with what's between my ears

Rather than between my legs and

Ignore the beg of my clit for immediate attention

Not to mention the unquenchable thirst of my skin for your touch

It's ..it's...much too hot and I've got to get these dishes washed

So I do the best I can but man...

The wet of my hands

Can't compare to the wet

Between my thighs

I sigh and then stop...

Dropped what I was about to rinse

When I sense your presence just inches

From me

But I don't turn

I just relish in the slow burn of body heat between us

You brush your fingers along my spine then wind your arms around my waist

Seal the space and make contact with my back and slowly

Sweetly

Kiss me

On my neck

His (Welcum Place)

He wanted to get lost in me

And still be in control…at the same time

So I wrapped him in my chocolate thighs

Looked into his eyes and spoke away the lies of the day

With the truth of our silence;

Breathed & sighed as he moved inside of me

Slowly….arduously filling my depths

While feeling my wet

He licks a single bead of sweat from my neck and

And I let go so that he knows

When in the throes of bad day

When he has no say or no one wants to pay

Attention or lend an ear

He is lord and master here

That I have no fear of where he will lead me

I just follow…each command from his lips &

Every mandate of his hips

Trust completely in each thrust

& it's a must because I am the suture

That binds up the breech between present darkness

And a future bright with the promise of better days

I will love the hard times away with each rotation

And arch of my back

Attack any lack of self confidence with the evidence

Of its presence inside him

While he's inside me.

360 degree the power in his stroke

Into a language of moans that can be spoken to any broken parts of his soul.

He will loose in me his chaos and I will lose control

For him…and on him and around him

Surrounding him in the fluidity of what it means

To be Wel'cum'd…

Again….and ….Again

Twilight (Cum Inside)

It began

At twilight

In the waning light of night merging with day

We lay nestled in the black of satin sheets

Until the starless sky completely matched its hue

Our two eager to become one but we understand

The reward of patience is fuckin' amazin'....

Pun intended

so for a while, we share smiles and

Beguiling whispers of our intentions

Mentioning unmentionable behavior between

Savored kisses

And the hypnotic hisses of

Needle dancing over vinyl

The final glissando fades into the quiet of

Sighs and moans

And the whisper of hands roaming on warm skin

We indulge in a foray of foreplay

A sensual display of love-borne lust

That thrusts us into an ethereal wonderland

And

We dance heart to heart

Instead of cheek to cheek

And speak in body language

Languidly…

Repeating each phrase

Nothing lost in translation

With such patience we

Decipher lip licks

And breath hitches

Twitches and trembles

And respond with nimble tongues and fingers

That linger long on glistening flesh

To mesh out every ounce of pleasure

With measured precision

Vision blurred by sweat and tears

So we let our movements be guided by our ears

You hear a clear path to my soul

When you roll your tongue around my pearl

My world shifts when you lift my hips

To take deeper sips of me

Immersion therapy at its best

I crest and overflow but you know

There 's no rest for the weary

This is merely the prelude to the song

That will be written tonight

A slight change in position assists in my mission

To please

I ease my body down yours

Careful to explore every inch of chocolate skin

That presents itself for inspection

Then I bring your body into subjection

With a torturously slow suck-session of licks and

deep throating

until you're bucking and coating my palate

with your sweetness

then you press your hips to mine

and find your way inside and I ride

each stroke

sing each note you provoke with your grind

the timbre of my voice constantly reminding you

whose it is

it's Yours not just now but every day

It's Yours baby…nobody else can ever have me this way

Mind, soul, and body

Papi, you got me

Now cum with me

Now

Cum with me

Now Cum

Inside my

Love

Open

You realized there's something special in store

The moment that you walked through the door

lights dim slim shadows cast by candles

handle hypnotic undulation perfectly

you hear me….

calling to you over soft seductive phonogram serenade

music played only for the sacred hours of lovemaking

painstakingly slow….

but just the right tempo for moans to be born

and from the corner comes the aroma of vanilla incense

this night promises intense pleasure

so with measured steps, you follow the carnal tug of my voice

uttering your name

but you came to a standstill

when the vision filled your eyes

garter kissed thighs…

satin bow tied tight at the top of fishnets

and who could forget the 5 inch leather heels

a revealing teddy no panties…

Sweet!

I point to your seat and you take it

Your eyes watching the slow motion of my right hand

entranced by the way my fingers move with familiarity

over my body….

then you smile…knowingly

this is punishment…for the naughty way

you teased me over the phone

nasty whispers of how much you wanted me when you knew I wasn't alone

Left me wanting thee

with your voice haunting me..

so now. Baby, watch me touch what you want to touch

I see such longing in your eyes as I open my legs wide

and slide my fingers deep inside my 'wet'

my thumb literally plays me clit-orally

and visually I know I'm stunning

Your hands running over the bulge in your pants gave it away

and you say, "…fuck you"

and I know what to do cause I know what you mean

so I obey and lean….back

relax…and raise my legs…then

Spread my thighs wider

and my fingers plunge deeper

and I watch you watching me

steadily

gaze unwavering

the slow methodical movement of your tongue sliding across your lips

more than involuntary motion

but a promise of things to cum…

like the tell-tale arching of my back and my struggle to breathe

my eyes begging for release

"please..", whispered through moistened lips

"baby...please...", as my control slips

then you slip from your chair..crawl the short distance

and ask if you can taste me there...

and you do...

and I'm done

breath becomes shallow

as your tongue inscribes your name in the hallows of my soul

whittling your name from my throat in notes

the deaf can hear

and I fear I will go insane

from the reign of pleasure you nimbly inflict on my body

I'm crazy in love

and my emotions begin to flood my eyes with tears

just as my orgasm floods the sheets I clutch for dear life

my voice lost in the storm erupting deep inside me

but my lips move in an inaudible plea for mercy

but you show none

and your oral assault continues 'til I've become

love-drunk

and I hit my bump against your grind

and find the strength to pull you up

so I can lay you down

and the sound of your breathing's got me sprung

as much as the rhythm of your tongue

and you whisper

'can I cum inside'

and I see absolute lust in your eyes

then you repeat

'please let me cum inside'

and I see love come alive

so I straddle you and open wide

Take every solid inch inside

and ride the waves of ecstasy

rock you deeper inside of me

clench you tight like grips of vice

Nice and slow and

"uhmmRen...ohhh"

you grab my hips and flip the script

turn me beneath you with an intensity that rips

my soul in twain

yet with each retreat I whisper, "again..."

and you oblige

and my thighs quake from the pounding weight

of your hips

my nails grip your back

I arch my back

I'm thrown way back

in time cause your grind

is the shit of legends

then with one swing of your pendulum

I cu-cu-cum back to the future

(let no man refute your skillz)

and heat builds until I'm ready to

boil over once more

and this time I'm takin you with me through the doors

of bliss

a kiss for luck and we're on our way

as stray tears run down my face

and my heart races and anticipates

the encore to this magnificent performance

and I glance at my fingers

my juices still lingering

over my wedding band

this man

the ruler of my body

the lord of my passions

is the lover of my soul

and my goal is to spend my life

enjoying being his friend, his confidante, his vixen and his wife

Good Night

His skin smells like sex….

Infused with the lavender of my sheets and the vanilla of my body

Warm…and intoxicating

It permeates the air like some exquisite French parfum…

I think…you really should be able to buy this stuff in stores

His breath is ragged….but smooth

Sliding cool and silky across my shoulders

Signifying the familiar rhythm of sleep

I smile…eyes dreamily slipping towards slumber

As my mind rewinds and replays the many ways in which he loved me

All day

&

All Night

I purr as a blur of visions and sounds and feelings and emotions

Wind their way through my thoughts

Twitch slightly and involuntarily as I remember the abrasive tickle of his mustache

Against my thighs…and lips…and clit…and it

Gets me wet all over again

And I want to baptize him in my rivers all over again

And I want to scream his name all over again

Use expletives like sacred script 'cause I just can't contain myself again

No mere act of copulation..no this is love making…creating…forming…life-breathing

Unseating the corruption of past lovers and ushering in the sanctity of what love should be

Redemptive

Cleansing

A blessing of the highest order

I smile even broader as I slip into dreams knowing their sweetness can't compare to the reality

Given to me

And I whisper softly….goodnight

Can't Hide Love

You're not fooled by the calmness of my exterior

Though my gaze holds yours steadily

And the rise and fall of my chest is smooth...almost calculated

You see it....

The heat and desire pooling just beneath the surface of my cocoa skin

The faint traces of sweat forming subtly along my brow

You smile slyly at the quivering pulse point on my neck

And slowly lick your lips

The hitch in my breathing doesn't go unnoticed.

You speak...about everything and nothing

But I don't hear a single word you say

I just follow the hypnotic movement of your lips

Fighting the urge to touch them with butterfly fingers

Lick them with lithe tongue and then suck their honey brown fullness

Until you moan my name

I exhale

Only then realizing that I'd been holding my breath at the thoughts that weighed

So heavily on my mind that they left imprints that are taking much too long to fade

I want you

~And you know it~

In the best and the nastiest of ways

In the deep down low and ride you slow kinda ways

The back seat of a caddy "just f*ck me daddy!" kinda ways

In the up against the wall until the pictures all fall kinda ways

I want you

And from the look in your eyes

I can tell you

Want me

Too

Seduction

Full lips don't lie

What they imply with flicks of pink

Inks more honestly than my pen

The innuendo in my smile is invitation to drink the libation of

My mouth so deeply that my southern linguistics permanently paint your palate Carolina blue

My accent suits you…

And to

Answer the question in your fingers as they linger on the small of my back

I mean exactly what my eyes say

I am not afraid of what lies, barely checked, beneath your gaze

So let's cut to the chase…

Place your hands over my heart

And listen

You are an active part of the music there

Now slide your hands lower

Slower

Bolder

Now close your eyes

And let my moan be your guide

Don't be shy…

And really I…

I don't mean to be forward

I'm just urging you toward

The glorious light of my lust…rous love

Above the music

My muse's sick flow

Throws cupid's arrows

Slickly robed in words

I'm saying freak what you heard

Did you hear me?

Feel free to connect the dots

I've got all night, alright?

"We can dance now; hook up later

We can do whatever…." - Seduction by Usher

Rope Burn

Pinned tightly between

Your body

And the wall

Legs spread

Back, an inverted arch

wrists bound and you call… my name

as the tip of your tongue traces the refrain of my new favorite song

along my neck

you whisper , "don't ever forget: pleasure belongs here"

and the sheer sound of your voice

forces me to believe

You've got me

Blindfolded..

And I am focused on every nuance of your touch

You don't rush….

You ensure I register every brush of your fingers….the slick wet of your tongue

The moist warmth of your lips…the firm pressure of your thumb

Sloooowwwwwly

Rooollllling

My clit

And it's hard….

Not to beg for my release

to trust that you hear the silent pleas

that speak through the quivering of my lips

and tremor in my thighs

the whimpering of your name

cocooned between panted sighs

"please…", I whisper

And rock my wet against your thick

"baby..please" I almost cry…as my control starts to slip

You firmly but gently grip my hair….

And share your most intimate desires

And inquire of me my own

And I Moan….

"I wanna feel a soft rope burn…" – Rope Burn by Janet Jackson

2am

Make me speak…

My silence is invitation

A coy intimation of my desire to be woo'd

I'm not moved to rhyme

With no reason….

You hold my keys and

Know exactly where my lock is

Where my spot is

I've got this…

Rhythm…I'm just dying to give you

If you..

Gather me inch by inch

Wrench music from my soul

'til I lose control of my tongue

And melodies once hung in the back of my throat spill freely and coat

Your ears

With the most erotic utterances you will ever hear

Write my song in slow, deliberate strokes

Press a little harder 'til your ink soaks through the page

Sages say, "silence is golden"

But I am beholden to the brilliance of your blackness

Scribbled across my thigh

And I breathe

incessantly

From this space between 1 and 3

Just waiting for you to

Reach out to me

And make me

speak

Skin:

Closer

I need to feel the heat of your…..

Skin

Imagine it beneath the curious flick of my tongue

Among other things

I've dreamed of this night for, like, all my life

Body rife with passion

What you imagine can't compare to

What air and opportunity barely keep at bay

Just say the words….

So I can quench my thirst for the mocha cradled in the cleft of your chin

And every other inch of your skin

The ink of your tattoos whisper haikus that invite my finger tips to play

To trace my every fantasy in Sanskrit on the canvas of your derma

Abhinava kama sutra… Ohhhh the

Weight and warmth of your hands

On my hips

The soft and moist of your lips

The inaudible scream in the grip of my nails in your back

All paint a path to pleasure

Pooling in generous measure just beneath our skin

And it blends so perfectly when you're inside of me

When you're one with me…

*"All I wanna see you in is just skin"

*Skin by Rihanna

How Does It Feel

He said…

"sit"…

As he drew circles with his index finger on my wrists

Looked at me with the sweetest longing in his eyes

Licked his lips and sighed…

"sit"

And the word, it, danced in the air between us

Dripping with sensuality and lust

Just 3 little letters….

That when placed together

And poured from the mouth of One man

can shift the universe

I blink…then purse my lips…about to speak

But he…hushed me with his gaze

Let fingertips graze my thigh

Placed one foot between mine

Spread my legs apart

Pulled me closer…placed my hand over his heart

And said…"I insist…baby….

Sit…"

And I stood there

Staring at the chair

He sat in

Then straddled him

And obeyed

Made my descent slow

Couldn't hold back my cry

As I took all of him inside of me

And he just held me there

Perfectly still as I struggled for air

He filled me completely and then he stared

Into my eyes and dared to look deeper into my soul

And then he let the words roll from his lips between

Slow sips of my tongue…

"for real….baby….how does it feel? How does it feel"

And he….

Shifted his weight

Sending tiny earthquakes through my womb

Making the room spin

And I whisper in his ear.

That it feels like

Love….

Go Missin'

Move

Like honey on warm skin

Go in

Like breath deep in lungs

Plunge into the depths of abandon

Like no one

Is watching…but me

Be free

I like you wild

And wide open

I'm hopin' you lose yourself tonight

Disappear inside yourself under these lights

And I might be persuaded to shed inhibitions

And I could be convinced to give you permission

To slide inside my invisibility

To hide inside my vulnerability

Cum with me

Go missin'

Listen it's not my desire to encumber

And I know there's safety in numbers

But the 5 or 6

you came with

Can't f*** with

the 69 reasons it

Would behoove you

To groove to that exit

Stage right

It's alright

To go missin'

Sex Therapy Pt. 1

He is some kind of sweet

The way he…

dripped caramel from his fingertips

Between my parted lips

onto my waiting tongue

then he let some slip down my chin

to my neck

he whispered…"let me get that….for u" (he's funny that way…)

and I drew what felt like my last breath as he deftly

licked every drop from my skin

then sprinkled cinnamon-sugar on the damp spots…

the scent assaults my senses; my body tenses at his attention to detail

He kisses a trail from my chest to each breast

Goosebumps, like Braille mark the path. I'm impressed

By the way his fingers read the message.

He lets his intent reflect in his eyes

His handsome face reveals the hint of a smile

While he turns me over onto my belly

And, well, he pours chocolate liqueur into the small of my back

Drinks it slow in exactly the way I hoped he would

I could feel his hard against my wet

I wanted him right then, but he whispered "not yet"

turned me back over; looked me in my eyes

could see my unchecked passion as he parted my thighs

"beautiful", he sighed

and I tried to imagine what he sees

He makes me believe in my sensuality

Makes my "thick" feel like the shyt

Every time he looks at me

And kisses me

He's so fu**ing sexy to me

And oooh my dayum what's he doing to me?

Face planted firmly between my legs

And I beg for mercy or more, see

He's got me going crazy and falling to pieces

I arch and moan from the oral attack he unleashes

I can't free his name from my tongue

It is hung somewhere between here and eternity

He's telling me to breathe and it's easier said than done

A jolt runs up my spine and I lose my mind and I find his name

He makes the rain cum hard and steady

And he…rides out the storm in the warmth of my wet

The unrest he sets loose in me begets a

Cataclysmic eruption

An interruption in the space-time continuum

I keep screaming his name

I'm still creaming his face

He licks every trace of nectar from my pot

He doesn't stop until my trembling subsides

And he slides up to my lips and

Drips my caramel from his chin ..

In-between my parted lips

onto my waiting tongue…

and I am some

kind

of

sweet….

The Memory of Your Kiss

The memory of your kiss
Lingers upon my lips like sunshine in a summer sky
And I can still taste the hollow of your throat
My tongue memorizing, by rote, the quickening of your pulse when I
…kiss you there…
Your hands in my hair paired with my name on your breath
Multiplied by the depth and breadth of my love for you
And your love for me equal
Cellular memory that cannot be erased by time and circumstance
We know this dance too fluently and
The memory of your touch lingers upon my skin
Something akin to summer rain: Warm and wet
I can never forget us
Even when time and distance won't let us be
Within arm's reach
Our hearts breach the miles between
And in the absence of arms, our voices cling to one another
Tethered by the longing born from too many hours apart
We, artfully, paint our dreams upon the canvas of a future framed in uncertainty
But I'm certain, see, that there is a "we" that will remain
That will be unchanged
And that my name will still taste sweet upon your tongue
And your voice will still bid me "come" like a whispered sigh in the evening breeze
I believe that love will stay
Well into the nights where sense is made
Even past the dawning of better days
Long after memory fades
And reality comes to light.

Sex Therapy pt. 2

He kissed tears from my eyes

As my sighs subsided

It quieted the room

Enough for us to hear the tune on the radio

"For All We Know" by Donny Hathaway

And there we lay satisfied under love's spell

It smells like vanilla

Peppered with chocolate and cinnamon

So good that I wanted some right then and right there

I licked his lips, he whispered "Rare..."

And then lost the remainder of my name in our kiss

Hissed when I gently bit his bottom lip and then kissed his chin

My tongue begins an arduous trek down his neck to his chest

Nipples, erect, greet me there and I dare not pass them by

I apply warm vanilla oil with the tips of my fingers

In circular motions and then I linger there and with care I lick them clean

Savor the taste of vanilla that clings to his warm skin

And then I let more oil drip on his stomach; his pelvis; his thighs

It reminds me of how his tongue played organza A sharp melodies between mine

So I will take my time and thank him properly

My lips roam free across the canvas of his skin and his hips begin a slow undulation

In appreciation

We are making a sexual symphony

He is singing for me….my name in a breathless sigh

I hummmm for him as I take him deep inside my mouth

soulful licks….staggered breathing

tonguing; staccato …bathing…..teasing

as sweet honey drips from the rock

he rocks and I roll my tongue

slow thorough examination - tip to base

his face tells the story and now he

is singing louder – a song unrivaled by Rachmaninoff or Grieg

and I am eager to hear more before the coda

I slow the tempo but maintain the rhythm

My body singing the song with him

the gentle nuances of wet lips on rigid flesh

the sounds mesh with his moans and curses -

Soft expletives that lace the verses

I heard his voice chorus then change

 Melody climaxed and beautifully came…. To an ending

Sending re-verb through the spea-kers

Thick and hot like acid jazz

old school funk or masterblaster

and in the afterglow of this orchestral flow, when I've drunk his well dry

I lay by his side and kiss tears from his eyes

Until his sighs subside.

Touch

My hands crave your skin

Smooth beneath my fingertips

Butter in my palms

After The Morning After

Woke up in the cool of the early morning

Comfortable, still, in your warm embrace

Your face peaceful with a trace of a smile

Content from your adventures in my wild the night before

I am more than satisfied

Indeed, I am satiated

Overwhelmed to overflowing

Lying here naked in more than just a physical sense

I've spent my life trying to hide who I am

Trying to diminish my personality

By building up a dam between me and the world outside

But you came inside and, brick by brick, stone by stone, and stick by stick

Pulled down my stronghold and emptied my moat

Slay my dragons

And my dam broke

You were not frightened by the flood

Did not take back or withhold your love

Stood in my downpour with open heart

Open arms

And a willingness to chart the sea of my broken-ness

And I acquiesced to your desire to enter into my sacred space

Watched in awe as you approach the throne of my heart

Lay on your face and prayed for me

and then STAYED…for me. Didn't abandon me

never tried to flee when my seas got rough

just loved me enough to make the hard times fade…

We made love…

Long before last night

Long before I held you tightly within my walls

Long before calls of your name rang out into the sky

Before I cried out to my Creator

Or made your hands grip the back of head

While I knelt before you between your legs

Before you proved to be a cunni-linguistic master

Before our smiles gave way to laughter gave way to sighs gave way to moans

You'd already made a home in my soul

Made love to me by getting to know my mind and my dreams

And all of the many things that make me…Rare

And I dare to believe that this is just the beginning.

I'm encouraged to believe that you and I are never ending

We are infinity like the seamless bands we placed on each other's fingers

Like the presence of the ancestors whose memories ever linger

I sing your praises to the morning sky as I lie next to you

Nothing left to do

But love

Moon (Extensions)

We lie

Wrapped in sky

Bathed in moonlight

Our dark in its brightness

And the slightest breeze teases me

Like his breath

Leaving me breathless

Cosmic conflict

Raging in veins

Silence, in vain, attempts to restrain

My cry

Starbursts behind my eyes

Leave me blind

But I can see

3rd eye open completely

Begetting the gift of intersensory

Perception

Clairvoyant reception – excellent

It is evident

What is cumming

And it is me

And it is us

We've coupled our energy

And transformed lust

Into lunar rainbow

An ethereal white glow

Dancing upon our skin

As we enter in-to

Multidimensional pleasures

We take measures to stem

The tide but inside a monsoon

Triggered by the moon and his movement

Is eminent

Is too intense to withstand

And I understand, now, black holes

Because the whole of my black soul

Quakes and implodes

Synergistic overload

My star bursts and slowly dies

And then is rebirthed through your borning cry

I'm reminded of my name in your tantric chant

And I can't remember any time but now

I try to speak but I don't know how

So I just

Wrap us in sky, and hold you tight

Until the last strains of pale moonlight

Give way to the illumination of dawn

The veil of memories now gone

I see you, dimly, in the light of the sun

Your perfect clarity, I , now, know only comes

In the light of the moon.

Look...Listen

Your eyes are speaking

Promises of things to come

I listen closely...

The Kiss

He looked through my too brown eyes

and not-so-perfect skin

directly into my soul

stepped closer into my

comfort zone 'til my world was thrown off kilter

He filtered out my excuses and explanations

and with a surgeons precision patience

He found me

Carved through this caricature to find my character

and then after a long moment I averted my eyes

'cause he'd seen through my disguise

and I was naked

My sacred spaces were hidden no more

and my imperfections lay scattered on the floor

of my cutting room

Doomed to be known in their entirety

and then silently he

lifted my chin

looked into those too brown eyes again

butterflies in my stomach dance and spin

heartbeats flutter and pound within

As he gently pulled me by my too thick waist

and placed his lips on mine

took his time inhaling my exhales

my thoughts failed as he

drank me in sips

slowly tasted my lips

savored their too full decadence

and I lost sense of time

as he reminded me that I was woman

and from inside I heard music

as he licked the lining of my mouth

I moan deliciously "uhmm" when he

suckles my bottom lip just before he dips

inside and my tongue guides him into the safety of my palate

And I caress him there as he strokes my hair

and I know beyond doubt

that I am loved.

Slow

My body needs you

Craves you with an urgency

That, urgently, needs your attention

And it's my intention to quench this deep down body thirst

But first

Just stand there

While I stare into your eyes

And try to surmise the feel of your fingertips on my bare skin

Where do I begin

Do I kiss you here or touch you there

I swear, my lips and tongue hardly know which way to go

I just know

It must be slow

I want it slower… slower… slower …..hold…

It right there

Don't you dare move

You've got me trembling on the edge of ecstasy

Back arching…I can barely breathe

I need you to whisper your intent into my ear

Kiss away the singular tear that rolls down my cheek

Greet my moan with your mouth

Swallow any doubt left lingering on my lips

Grip my hips

And go deep

Keep your name on repeat

From between my clenched teeth

Guttural…from my throat but take note

You got to go slowwwww

I need it slower… slower… slower… hold

Not yet… make me wait for it

Mouth open

Body trembling

Make me beg for it

Stroke deliberately

Change up rhythmically

Take your time

With that grind

Look what you did to me

My nails in your back

Heart and legs open wide

I take every single inch of your love and lust inside

And I

Tighten my grip

feel your control slip

And whisper, "cum with me…"

You oblige

We arrive

As moans give rise to screams melt into sighs give way to silence

The evidence of our lovemaking fresh on our skin

We blend into tangled sheets;

 Awash in afterglow

Glad that we know

The reward of taking it slow….

Hold…

Exhale...

Pamela "RareEpiphany" Best lives in Atlanta, GA with her son James. She is also the author of "Of Love: The Poetry of RareEpiphany" and an accomplished jazz vocalist with 3 cds to her credit. She enjoys spending time with family, community service for the homeless, and performing poetry and music around the country.

Made in the USA
Columbia, SC
30 November 2023